The Next Chapter

Theresa Radley

 BookLeaf Publishing

Presentation by *BookLeaf Publishing*

Web: www.bookleafpub.com

E-mail: info@bookleafpub.com

ISBN: 9789357441926

First edition 2023

Mom, this is for you. It's because of you I started writing. I love you.

For my kids, for helping me redefine my purpose. The last three poems are for you.

To my younger self for all the lessons you had to learn, all the times your heart had to break, for all the pain you endured. No matter what you made it through. Thank you for telling our story.

ACKNOWLEDGEMENT

First and foremost, I have to thank Tonda, my best friend, for encouraging me to accept the challenge and create the project, helping to make my dream a reality, and always being my "go-to." You are the true definition of a best friend and I'm so grateful for our friendship.

A huge shoutout to my mom, for being my first fan, who gave me this gift of writing, and constantly encourages me to write happy poems.

Thank you, Carrie, for being one of the first to read every poem and to show an abundance of support.

And thank you to Branden for our writing challenges and writing session, for being an inspiration and a muse, for believing in me before I did, and for showing me the definition of love.

PREFACE

For most of my life, I suffered from anxiety and depression. I hid it from everyone, including myself. Yet, with every poem, I had to face the truth. I've experienced some low points in my life, and no matter what, poetry was part of the healing process.

In the past year, I've spent a lot of time reflecting, growing, and falling in love with every aspect of myself. This is a preview of my highs and lows, my story, and my journey into the next chapter of my life.

Empty

Feeling empty
Like my tank is on E
There is nothing in the cup
I have nothing to give
Everyone just keeps taking
And they give nothing
I don't dare complain
Or even try to explain

I'm at a lost
I feel stuck
Like I'm a message in a bottle
Floating in an ocean
of loneliness and disappointment
My words will never be heard

I'm drowning in my thoughts
Desperately trying to catch my breath
The voices won't be quiet
I'm struggling to grasp for air
With feelings of despair
My lungs are getting tighter
My heartbeat is getting weaker

I'm so close to breaking
Shattering into a million pieces
Like a fallen glass or broken mirror
It's a never-ending spell of bad luck
I'm down at my worst
And there's no hope for a better tomorrow
It's pointless like an unsharpened pencil

I'm emotionless and fragile
Please just let me be

Strength

She is barely holding on
Desperately trying to be strong
You wouldn't know
Because she doesn't let it show

Each day she's in a battle
A constant difficult struggle
To keep putting up the fight
To keep doing what's right

She hides behind the sunshine
But she is dying inside
She continues to mask her pain
Causing her a tremendous strain

She's drowning in her sorrows
So afraid of another tomorrow
Another day of neglect and hurt
Of never feeling she's enough

She knows she's loved
But most days she feels alone
The doubt and insecurities
Make it impossible for her to see
All of who she's meant to be

She's tired of the never-ending cycle
Fighting for survival
pretending she's fine
Fake smiling all the time

If you only knew
All of what she's been through

People tell her she's strong
But most days she's barely holding on

Illusion

What we had was like a dream
No, call it a nightmare
Because of the pain you caused
Left some serious deep scars
I'm reminded of the mistakes I made
Letting you back in time and again
Thinking it would be different
Somehow you've changed
But the pain would hit harder
As you showed it didn't matter

I loved you and idolized our love
While I was an image, a facade
The one you had to never feel lonely
The one who boosted you up
You used me constantly for your own gain
Taking my energy, leaving me drained
But to you, I gave and gave again

I was swept up in the little things
The way you smiled and held me tight
Didn't care that you didn't treat me right
That you kept all these secrets
Including your feelings for me

And now that you are gone
I have nothing left but shame
Why did I play your games
Why did I allow you to treat me this way
Why did I think this was okay
Why did I believe you were all I deserved
Why is it taking so long to heal

Breaking the Pattern

It may be hard to admit
But truthfully I'm used to it
Your actions are a pattern
Showing nothing matters
But your needs and desires
You are filled with an evil fire
You stomp around with demands
Shouting out your commands
Not stopping until they are met
I fear all of your threats
You think you have all the answers
But you are destructive like cancer
Your wrath continues to multiply
And I'm over questioning why

I continue to attempt to please
But none of it comes with ease
You believe I'm not enough
Say it's impossible to measure up
My strength only motives you more
To come harder than before
To fight me with such power
Screaming louder and louder
They tell me not to be a coward
But I'm damaged by our encounters

Yet, maybe in some way I've given up
I've truly had enough
This relationship isn't worth saving
And this game I'm done playing
Don't take my silence for weakness
Because I know I'm filled with greatness
I've come to fully understand
You'll never fit in my master plan
To be the best version of me
This is not my vision of family

Yes, I allowed your words to hurt
I was always jumpy and alert
Terrified of your next strike
And never ready to fight
But that will no longer be my life
I'm standing up for what's right
You no longer have any form of control
I'm taking back what you stole

Time

Our time is not guaranteed
Never know when it's time to leave
We need to make the most
Of everything life has to offer
In the blink of an eye
Life can pass us by

We all know this to be true
But how much do you follow the rules
Do you seize every day like it's your last
Or do you live stuck in the past
Stressing over things out of your control
Wasting time until God calls you home
Do you spend your days with gratitude
Or are you consumed by a negative attitude
Do you show people how much you care
Making it obvious love is there

I ask these questions because
Of my own struggle with the answers
I try to take on each day with pride
Moving forward with positivity in my stride
But truthfully most days it's not easy
To always be filled with positive energy
I know I've made a lot of mistakes

And have had my share of heartbreaks
But I want to live more in the presence
Believing how much each day is a present

It's clear that the clock will keep on ticking
So while I'm still alive and kicking
I'm going to keep on smiling
And climbing and stringing
I'm going to achieve all my goals
And make the most of my roles
When it's my time to leave earth
I don't want to have any regrets
I will have achieved what I set out to do
I will have stayed loyal and true

I hope you choose to do the same
Instead of dishing out the blame
Take life into your own hands
And put action into those plans
Stop chasing the money and wealth
Start focusing on your health
Know its not cash flow that makes you rich
But how you followed your niche
How you surrounded yourself with positivity
And helped out in the community
It's the love that you expressed for others
And learning what really matters

Poet

Sometimes I don't feel like a poet
Because I don't always show it
I have so many emotions
Can't always get them in a poem

Thoughts float in my brain
Exploring the joy and pain
I got so much to explain
But sometimes it's a strain

Sometimes verses flow easy
Others the block gets the best of me
I try to write every day
Because I have so much to say

Want to use my words to inspire
Help others fuel their desire

But sometimes I'm too shy to publicize
Worried about the criticize
But then my voice will never be heard
And that will be absurd

Emotions

"Emotions are reactions
To our past interactions"
It's never about our current situation
Or the immediate conversation
It's the pent-up frustration
And the overwhelming tension
It's never truly being able to heal
From the way the experience made us feel

Cause and effect
Leaves us with a defect
Repeating the same mistake
Allowing the heart to break
Accepting this is the way to feel
Instead of allowing time to heal

We continue in the same cycle
Avoiding reality, sulking in denial
We continue to let the past haunt us
Never being able to trust
Shutting down even though it's not right
Not willing to fight, just living in the flight

Feelings blaring in overdrive
Not sure how to survive

It becomes hard to breathe
Trying to set your mind at ease
Praying for the strength
Take one deep breath

Inhale, exhale, repeat
Needing something concrete
Before I accept defeat

Mixed Signals

It's not goodbye
It's see you later

I said I could be patient
That I could wait
Stand by your side
As you cleared your mind
When you fixed up loose ends
We could be more than friends

But it's too much of a sacrifice
A true inconvenience
All of the inconsistency
Never enough efficiency
I need stability

Our moments together are perfection
But our time apart brings out too much emotion

I can't pretend like I don't care
That I don't want you near
That I don't think of you all the time
Wishing you could be mine

I'm trying to give you your space
But that's not the case
One minute I can go with the flow
The next I'm chasing after your soul

Truth is I need to let you go
Stop sending mixed signals
Because I'm just as confused
Still healing from previous abuse

So wishing you all the best
Hoping you pass all of lives tests
Sending you luck and support
And nothing but positive thoughts

Expectations

My expectations are impossible to meet
I want to be more than swept off my feet
It's not just all about wine and dine
Or being intrigued by mind
Or our bodies being perfectly in-sync
It's being able to know what I think

It's all of the little things
From the good morning rings
To the late night texts
And listening to my requests
It's knowing what I need
Yet sometimes letting me take the lead
It's holding me accountable
And always being ready to snuggle
It's knowing when I need my space
And when I need your embrace
It's providing a sense of security
But letting me still do me
It's an undeniable companionship
That's deeper than friendship
Building a solid foundation
Ready to overcome any confrontation
It's being spontaneous and romantic
And not overreacting when I get dramatic

It's accepting all of my emotions
And reading all of my poems
It's showing up even when I don't ask
Making me comfortable removing my mask
It's slow dancing to an R&B beat
And making me feel complete
It's all this and so much more
I want a love like never before

Independent Baggage

My experiences leave me drained
I'm tired and often ashamed
Of this journey we call life
I wonder, did I do anything right

I carry around a heavy burden
Yet, I'm still determine
To never let you know my damage
Positivity is my advantage

I march with a sense of pride
Never letting you destroy my stride
I've overcome battles on my own
So I walk my path alone

I don't often ask for help
I can do life by myself
I've tried to trust in others
And feel like I'm a bother

Please don't be offended
My torched path leaves me guarded
Yet I feel like I've been rewarded

My baggage is extremely heavy
But for me, it is a victory
It has become my identity

It's a symbol of the overcame obstacles
Of surpassing all of my struggles
Of surviving my hardest troubles
Of standing on top of the rumble

My anxiety challenges me to quit
Says breakdown this is it
But my faith restores my light
And I stand ready to fight

Maybe soon I'll let you carry a load
Help me on this road
For now I'll hold on to my luggage tight
Waiting for the next flight

Warrior

I've been knocked down
But never knocked out
I'll always keep getting up
I'll always keep pushing on

Each day I'm in my fighting stance
Ready to destroy the battles
Conquer the obstacles
And rise to the top

I'm the rainbow after a perfect storm
The light at the end of the tunnel
The diamond in the rough

My pain has always fueled the fire
My desire leads me to success
Each day is a stepping stone
To achieve the victory I deserve

Don't ever count me out
Because I never give up

Positive Energy

God made me different
I'm not a product of my environment
The pain doesn't make me bitter
The hurt only makes me stronger
No matter what I've been through
I still stay authentic and true

I watch people become more guarded
More afraid of good love
Constantly worried about their downfall
Never trusting in love at all
It's a shame to witness
Living in pain, minimizing the bliss
I know evil exists
But I'm determined good wins this

Call me way too optimistic
But I'll never be pessimistic
There's way too much beauty in the world
And too many lessons I've learned
To go against God's plan
There are things I don't need to understand

I take each hardship as a lesson
Yes, sometimes it triggers my depression

But I have to find the positive
And become a bit more proactive
There are opportunities I won't let go by
Positive energy manifests positive energy

You can say, I trust way too easy
And yes, I'll agree
Even though it has caused me pain,
I'll never change
My smile will only get brighter.
Best believe I was born a fighter

Cheers

Cheers to all of me!
And every battle I've overcome
Cheers to the one who didn't believe
That I'd ever achieve
Cheers to overcoming obstacles
And doing the impossible
Cheers to wiping away tears
And getting over my fears
Cheers to solving conflicts
And taking necessary risks

Cheers to finding victory
And being the best version of me
Cheers to shutting out the insecurity
And accepting all of my identities
Cheers to learning to love myself
And having a positive self esteem

Cheers to never looking back
While learning from my past
Cheers to keep moving forward
And thanking those who supported

Cheers to my community
Who have shown me unity

Cheers to the ones by my side
Who are my life lines
Cheers to every aspect of my life
Feeling truly blessed!

Complex

There's this puzzle I don't understand
My fingers fit perfectly in your hands
You hold my heart with such grace
Butterflies with each embrace
Every part of my being screams to be yours
But there are moments I feel torn

I get caught up in my past
Fearful you and I won't last
Afraid to give love another chance
Yet longing for your romance

you feel the same as I do
You question is too good to be true
Can this be the happily ever after
Or another tragic disaster
You fear I'll disappear again
And we won't even be friends
We both admitted we lack trust
So I ask is this love or just lust

I've never wanted anything so much
I'm obsessed with your touch
I see my future in your eyes
As you rub and tickle my thighs

I keep putting back up my guard
Covering up past wounds and scars
So tempted to take the leap
Put my trust in fate
Free me from any hesitation
Give in to all the temptation

Part of me feels like what do I have to lose
I'm already so much in love with you
I've already given in to you before
What's the harm in once more
I need to let go of labels and titles
Stop wasting time living in denial
Give into you once more
And this time let our love soar

Poetry

I see the lyrics in your eyes
Hear the beat in your soul
Together we are the perfect melody
Like that Sunday music mamma played
An ideal blend of heaven
Pure perfection
I feel the rhythm with each touch
Knowing I can't get enough
Let me put this on repeat
And sing you again and again

Love

They say love is about sacrifice
And I don't mean to patronize
I just don't see the truth in your lies

I think love is dangerous
I question its purpose
It makes me highly nervous

I believed I felt its presence
But I was blinded by my innocence
And had to survive in its absence

Love has been more of an obstacle
A constant struggle
Feeling like I'm always in trouble

But now that you are in my universe
And I've fallen in love with your poetry verse
My thoughts on love are in reverse

I want to express on a canvas, to illustrate
The beauty of what you helped me create
While my feelings for you inflate

You've become someone I adore

I want to give you me and so much more
With you, I want to explore

So maybe love is a sacrifice
And I won't even think twice
Having you as my lover
Is it worth the danger
I want to be wrapped in your presence
And always embrace your essence
With you, we will conquer all obstacles
And know anything is possible
You have become my universe
And made my smile luminous
Let's continue to write, to illustrate
To show our love is great
You are the one I adore
And there's nothing I want more

Other Half

Never understood the term, other half
Said I wanted to be complete on my own
Didn't need a partner to achieve
I was dope just being me
I wasn't broken and needed to be fixed
I struggled but yet I had this

I claimed to be whole
Said I could do this life solo
But you've captivated my soul
This isn't about power or control
This goes against what I was told
Don't give no man my heart to hold

See you're everything I never knew I needed
My expectations you've exceeded
And with you I know I've succeeded
Our hearts beat in sync
We know what each other thinks
Your happiness matters
Want to be in each of your chapters

The way you challenge and encourage me
Your support is a guarantee
And for you I'll do the same

By your side even without fortune and fame
Every day with you is another lesson
Each moment is a blessing

Yes, on my own I achieve what I desire
But together we are fire
You make me want to exceed my potential
Your love is influential
Even though I can, I won't do this without you
This is that love they call true

Be

Be my conductor, take me on the ride of my life
Be the one who treats me right

Be my composer and arrange my soundtrack
Be the one who always has my back

Be my handyman and fix what's broken
Be the one I've chosen

Be my teacher by expanding my knowledge
Be the one I pay homage

Be my accountant as we build our finances
Be the one to hold me tight as we dance

Be my chef, preparing me a healthy meal
Be the one who keeps it real

Be my doctor, take care of my needs
Be the one to take the lead

Be my pillow as I drift off to sleep
Be the one to never make me weep

Be my diary where I can share my secrets

Be the one to make me believe in it

Be my friend building a strong foundation
Be the one with a deep connection

Be my sky lit by the stars
Be the one to eliminate the scars

Be my dreams, so everything has come true
Be the one I pursue

Be my bartender, serve up a nice drink
Be the one to make me think

Be my personal trainer, help me get fit
Be the one to make me commit

Be my publicist, market my success
Be the one to ease my stress

Be my hype man encouraging me every step of
the way
Be the one to put me on display

Be my lyrics to every poem I write
Be the one I snuggle with at night

Be my laughter when I need it most
Be the one to hold me close

Be my last first kiss
Be the one I can't resist

Be my heart and soul
Be the greatest love I've ever known

For my Daughter

A dream I wasn't supposed to have
Odds were against me
As they placed this angel into my arms
Turned my life upside down
And taught me lessons I could never understand

Rules made to protect her
a bond getting stronger
Praying to make all the right moves
teach her how to handle life's greatest challenges
And pray to show her to be strong brave and
confident

The pressure to raise this baby girl into a woman
Gets exciting and challenging every day
As she grows into her independence
Although she's like me in so many ways
I'm blessed she has qualities
I'll never have

My diva, my rock star, my blessing
I'll watch you fight the status quo
Go against the stereotypes
Be a princess, an athlete, and a woman with
strength

As you take on the world with confidence
Pushing through every obstacle
Standing up for what's right
And empowering them all to see
It's a woman's world
We will win this fight

Sunshine

His little hand holds mine
I wish I could stop time
And forever experience this joy
This moment with my baby boy

His smile is so bright
Hes my little knight
Always ready to put up a fight
And do what's right

Hes captured my heart
From the very start
His humor is contagious
He's quite courageous

He wasn't part of my plan
And most days I struggle to understand
How I got to be so lucky
That he calls me mommy

He is my lifeline
He is my sunshine

Number 3

My sweet little number three
You truly saved me
For you I wanted to be better
You deserved a good mother

As you lay in my arms
I pray I can protect you from harm

Every twist in turn in my life
Led me to that beautiful smile
Your energy keeps me going
And gives me hope and courage
Every day you show us
There aren't obstacles
Your determination is inspiring
You love to sing, dance and to read
I see the qualities you got from me

My sweet little number three
You are the best part of me
I've made many mistakes
But bringing you into this world
Is not one of them

You are my reminder

That the greatest blessings
Come from our darkest days